Clever Trevor
knows his animals

ALAN ROGERS

GRAFTON BOOKS
A Division of the Collins Publishing Group

LONDON GLASGOW
TORONTO SYDNEY AUCKLAND

Clever Trevor knows a ...

cat

The cat's having fun

What's the dog done?

Which one is the cow?

Clever Trevor knows a ...

sheep

Where's the sheep now?

Clever Trevor knows a ...

pigeon

The pigeon's in the street

The snake sings S-S-Silent Night

Clever Trevor knows a ...

mouse

The mouse keeps out of sight

Clever Trevor knows an …

too-woo

owl

The owl wakes up at night

Clever Trevor knows a ...

tiger

The tiger's in the jungle

He's not scared of the scarecrow

Grafton Books
A Division of the Collins Publishing Group
8 Grafton Street, London W1X 3LA

Published by Grafton Books 1986
Copyright © Alan Rogers 1986

British Library Cataloguing in Publication Data

Rogers, Alan, *1952*-
Clever Trevor knows his animals.——(Clever
Trevor books)
1. Animals——Juvenile literature
I. Title
591   QL49

ISBN 0-246-12846-1

Printed in Belgium by
Henri Proost & CIE PVBA